POLICE IN WHITE FACE

The Killing of Tyre Nichols

BARTON WADE

Copyright © 2024 Barton Wade
All rights reserved
First Edition

Fulton Books
Meadville, PA

Published by Fulton Books 2024

ISBN 979-8-88982-419-0 (paperback)
ISBN 979-8-88982-420-6 (digital)

Printed in the United States of America

CHAPTER 1

THE BIRTH

Tyre Nichols was a twenty-nine-year-old Black man born in Sacramento, California, to RowVaughn Wells. The youngest of four siblings and lived with his mother and stepfather, Rodney Wells, in Memphis, Tennessee. Not long after moving to Memphis, he started a job alongside his stepfather at FedEx. He had only been working there for nine months before he was killed. Interviewing a coworker, it was said he was a beloved employee at his job and carried a smile everywhere he went. From a child up until adulthood, he was a passionate skateboarder and photographer. These hobbies he engaged in during his downtime on weekends. He once posted on his photography page that photography helps him look at the world in a more creative way, and it expresses him in ways he cannot write down to people. Tyre Nichols was pulled over on January 7 at or about 8:30 p.m. for reckless driving while coming home from Shelby Farms, a local park, after taking photos. During the whole interaction with Tyre, he was beaten and died three days later in a hospital. May his passion continue as he lay in the arms of the Lord.

CHAPTER 2

THE MOTHER

RowVaughn Wells's Response
after Tyre Nichols's Death

His mother recalls the morning three days before her son's death. She said she had been preparing chicken for dinner that afternoon and planned to cook it his favorite way. She stated that Nichols was coming from Shelby Farms, a local park where he liked to go and take pictures of the sunset. She states it's just hard for her to even fathom all of this because it's not real to her right now. She states she just wanted people to remember her son as a "beautiful soul." As a father of two, a girl and a boy, I can relate to the feeling of a mother's love for her son. I cannot imagine anything happening to my son. It would totally destroy my wife. There is no love like a mother's love for her son. That is because the bond between a mother and son is unweave. No father can ever break that bond. No matter how much he loves his father, his love and devotion are to his mother no matter how she lives her life. That is a fact that not too many people can dispute. 2Pac said it all in his song "Dear Mama." So, Mama Wells, don't despair; you will see your son again when the Lord chooses that time to come.

CHAPTER 3

THE ALLEGED MURDERS

Tadarrius Bean

Tadarrius Bean, twenty-four, from Olive Branch, DeSoto County, Mississippi. Bean graduated from the University of Mississippi with a criminal justice degree. The five-foot-ten-tall man completed his graduation in May 2020. Prior to that, in 2016, he graduated from Center Hill High School in Olive Branch where he also played football. He was hired by Memphis Police Department in Memphis, Shelby County, Tennessee, in August of 2020, the same year he graduated. He is unmarried.

Emmitt Martin III

Emmitt Martin III is a thirty-year-old Black man. He was hired by Memphis Police Department in March 2018. He went to Bethel University a Christian College in McKenzie, Tennessee, where he played tight end on the football team. He has one daughter and was described by a former Bethel University classmate as "one of the coolest brothers ever." Joshua Harper, who is now a pastor in Missouri, said he followed Martin on social media after they left the Christian College in McKenzie, Tennessee. He said Martin posted a lot about his daughter. He also said the man depicted in court papers "is not the person that he knows": "I was shocked only for a second because I understood that he was a police officer, and I know behind the badge that anything can happen when anyone has power and authority."

Desmond Mills Jr.

Desmond Mills Jr., thirty, was born in Hartford, Connecticut, and graduated from Bloomfield High School, class of 2008. He spent his formative years in a suburb north of Bloomfield. He went on to West Virginia State where he played football in the 2009–

2010 season where he played offensive guard and was given the nickname "Box." Mills was hired by Memphis Police Department in March 2017. One of his former coaches, Kip Shaw, said, "I'm not one to be surprised a lot. But when I saw the news, I was just shocked. I've been coaching for a long time, and you just never know."

A Timeline of the Investigation into His Death

The investigation into the death of Tyre Nichols in Memphis, Tennessee, continues. Nichols died several days after a violent encounter with five Memphis police officers, which was caught on camera. Here is a timeline of the events leading up to and surrounding his death.

January 7, 2023

Tyre Nichols, a twenty-nine-year-old Black man, was pulled over by police for alleged reckless driving. According to Nichols's mother, RowVaughn Wells, Tyre was two minutes away from his home when he was pulled over. Officers say they then pursued Nichols after he ran and apprehended him. Attorneys for Nichols's family said that Nichols originally cooperated with the officers. They say Nichols told police that "he was just trying to get home" from FedEx, where he worked, and yelled for his mother three times toward the end. Body camera footage shows the initial altercation. An officer warns Nichols "I'm going to beat your ass" and "I'm going to tase your ass" as various officers hold him on the ground and yell at him. Nichols's tone remains calm, at one point telling the cops, "You guys are really doing a lot right now." He manages to break free from the officers as they appear to try to deploy a stun gun on him, and he runs away. Several officers can later be seen in body camera footage grouped with Nichols, standing over him as he's on the ground. Two officers hold him down, and a third kicks him. A fourth officer comes over with a baton and the officers pick Nichols up from the ground and hold him up while officers appear to strike him in the face and torso. As Nichols falls to his knees, several officers kneel and lean over him while another appears to stand a few feet away, watching. Additional officers run into the frame. At least one officer kicked him in the head as Nichols appeared to have his hands behind his back. They eventually dragged him into the street and then leaned him against their vehicle. Nichols remains slumped next to the car for roughly twenty minutes, it appears, before officers' first attempt to render him aid. Several minutes later, EMTs appear to lean over Nichols before an ambulance appears. The footage shows officers beating Nichols and using pepper spray as he begins yelling for his mother, who lives nearby. He can be heard screaming "Mom" at least three times. The officers yell multiple times at Nichols to "give me your hands." The officer with the baton can be heard saying, "I've baton the fuck out of you," then appears to strike him on the back three times. Officers pull Nichols to a stand, then appear to punch and slap him. After the incident, Nichols "complained of having a shortness of breath" and was transported by ambulance to Memphis's St. Francis Hospital in critical condition, according to police. Due to Nichols's condition, the Shelby County District Attorney's Office was contacted, and TBI special agents were subsequently requested to conduct a use-of-force investigation, according to the TBI. The Memphis Police Department said at the time that "officers involved will be routinely relieved of duty pending the outcome of" the TBI's investigation.

January 10, 2023

Nichols died three days after being detained by Memphis police.

January 18, 2023

Kevin G. Ritz, United States attorney for the Western District of Tennessee, announced that the FBI and DOJ are investigating the incident. "State authorities have publicly announced that the Tennessee Bureau of Investigation is investigating," Ritz said in a statement. "In addition, the United States Attorney's Office, in coordination with the FBI Memphis Field Office and the Civil Rights Division of the Department of Justice, has opened a civil rights investigation."

January 20, 2023

The Memphis Police Department announced that it fired five police officers following an investigation into Nichols's death. The officers were identified as Tadarrius Bean, Demetrius Haley, Emmitt Martin III, Desmond Mills Jr., and Justin Smith. They are all Black men. "After a thorough review of the circumstances surrounding this incident, we have determined that five MPD officers violated multiple department policies, including excessive use of force, duty to intervene, and duty to render aid," the department said in a news release.

January 23, 2023

The video footage of Nichols's interaction with the five Memphis police officers was viewed by Nichols's family and attorneys. They described the video as "appalling" "deplorable," "violent," and "troublesome on every level," according to Ben Crump, attorney for the Nichols family. "What he was in that video was defenseless the entire time," said Antonio Romanucci, another attorney for the family. "He was a human piñata for those police officers. It was unadulterated, unabashed, nonstop beating of this young boy for three minutes." Romanucci also mentioned that Nichols, who died on January 10, was kicked during the footage. The family said they saw the police kick, pepper spray and use a stun gun on their son all while Nichols repeatedly asked, "What did I do!" This same week, Memphis Fire Department officials announced that two employees involved in the initial patient care of Nichols were relieved of duty and are being investigated for their role in the incident, according to an official statement given to ABC affiliate WATN.

January 26, 2023

A grand jury indicted the five officers involved in the Nichols incident. They each have been charged with murder and are in custody. They have been charged with "second-degree murder, and aggravated assault, aggravating kidnapping, resulting in bodily injury, aggravated kidnapping involving the possession of a weapon official misconduct through unauthorized exercise of police power and failure to act when there is a duty to do so."

Note: All five officers are out on bond and pleaded not guilty on February 17, 2023. An independent autopsy, completed by a forensic pathologist hired by the family's attorneys, found that Nichols suffered from "extensive bleeding caused by severe beating," according to the family. "His observed injuries are consistent with what the family and attorneys witnessed on the video of his fatal encounter with police on January 7," the family of Tyre Nichols and their attorneys said in a statement. "Further details and findings from this independent report will be disclosed at another time." Memphis chief of police Cerelyn Davis called the officers' actions "heinous, reckless and inhumane," adding that "when the body camera footage is released in the coming days, you will see for yourself." She also stated she expects protests following the video's release but warns that even though she anticipates outrage, "none of this is a calling card for inciting violence."

January 27, 2023

Memphis officials released the footage of Nichols' confrontation with police. Four videos were shared on Vimeo by the city of Memphis. The city shared footage from three body-worn cameras, as well as a pole camera, amounting to about sixty-seven minutes total. One clip is a city surveillance video, which shows Nichols being hit, kicked, and punched by several of the officers, including the use of a baton. Another clip is a body camera video, which shows the officers beating Nichols. Another clip highlights audio in which Nichols can be heard yelling out "Mom!" several times. The clip later captures Nichols slumped on the ground next to a vehicle. "Like so many, I was outraged and deeply pained to see the horrific video of the beating that resulted in Tyre Nichols's death. It is yet another painful reminder of the profound fear and trauma, the pain, and the exhaustion that Black and Brown Americans experience every single day," President Joe Biden said in response to the footage.

Note: Shelby County sheriff Floyd Bonner Jr. also launched an internal investigation into two deputies who appeared on the scene and have relieved them of duty pending the investigations and findings.

January 30, 2023

Memphis police officer Preston Hemphill, an officer involved in the Tyre Nichols traffic stop, and one unidentified officer were relieved of duty during an ongoing investigation, according to Memphis police. Hemphill, who is White, and the other officer were relieved of their duties on January 8, 2023, according to the Memphis police. Hemphill was later fired on February 3, 2023. Hemphill allegedly deployed his Taser during the confrontation. In his own body camera video, Hemphill is seen chasing Nichols down the road but then turns back to the scene of the initial traffic stop. Hemphill was heard on his body camera video saying twice, "I hope they stomp his ass. The Memphis Fire Department also announced that three members who were deployed in an ambulance to the scene after the beating have been fired. EMTs Robert Long and JaMicheal Sandridge, who initially assessed Nichols at the scene, were fired for failing "to conduct an adequate patient assessment of Mr. Nichols," according to the fire department. MFD Lt. Michelle Whitaker, who was inside the first ambulance at the scene, was also fired. Hemphill was fired for "truthfulness and violation for not using the taser in compliance with regulation."

February 7, 2023

One of the former officers, Demetrius Haley, took a photo of "obviously injured" Nichols after the beating and admitted sharing them with other officers in the department, including a civilian employee, and a civilian female acquaintance, which readily admitted. The action violated a Memphis police policy regarding confidential information, which states that officers cannot share information relating to official police matters "without prior approval or subpoena, except to authorized persons. Seven additional officers could face discipline in connection with the incident. Those additional officers will be receiving a "statement of charges," which notifies an officer about a policy violation prior to an administrative hearing. The investigation in this case is ongoing, and charges may change.

POLICE IN WHITE FACE

ABOUT THE AUTHOR

I was born in Burlington, North Carolina, on April 19, 1958, with three other brothers and two sisters. I graduated from Ashworth College with a bachelor's degree in criminal justice. I am retired from the US Army and am a federal police officer with twenty-eight years of law enforcement. I am married with two kids and live in Atlanta, Georgia.

www.ingramcontent.com/pod-product-compliance
Lightning Source LLC
Chambersburg PA
CBHW031641170726
47990CB00018B/1625